D0760807

CALGARY PUBLIC LIBRARY

NOV   2011

THE NEW FRENCH INTERIOR

THE NEW FRENCH INTERIOR

Penny Drue Baird

THE MONACELLI PRESS

To my mom, Terri Baird, a pioneer in design, who trained me from
a tender age to have an eye for everything tasteful.

Copyright © 2011 Penny Drue Baird and The Monacelli Press,
a division of Random House, Inc.

All rights reserved.

Published in the United States by The Monacelli Press, a division
of Random House, Inc., New York

The Monacelli Press and the M logo are registered trademarks
of Random House, Inc.

Library of Congress Control Number: 2011926462

ISBN: 978-1-58093-310-0

10 9 8 7 6 5 4 3 2 1

Designed by Susan Evans, Design per se, Inc.

Printed in China

www.monacellipress.com

CONTENTS

THE NEW FRENCH INTERIOR

E verything old is new again, as the saying goes. In interior design and architecture, as in fashion, just about everything can be traced back to a historical precedent. While fashion is affected by seemingly fleeting trends, interior design evolves very slowly. Nevertheless, homes do evolve as do people, both in their tastes and lifestyles. What appeals to young couples on the path to adulthood is likely to change as they navigate through parenthood and eventually become empty nesters.

France has been a leader in taste and fashion for hundreds of years. So many of our contemporary furnishings have been influenced by French design in one way or another that it is practically impossible not to see a gesture to French design when one analyzes the line or look of an object.

Historically, French design was based on the styles popular with the reigning monarch of the time. Frenchmen copied, to the best of their ability, the styles popular with the king and his court. As monarchs came into power and as generations passed, the bourgeoisie and middle classes would find themselves copying the new king's style. After centuries of what we, today, group together in a loose category called "traditional," the dawn of the twentieth century rang in new ideas philosophically and in reality.

By definition, whatever era we are living in is "modern." One has only to look at the flappers of the 1920s to see that they thought of themselves as terribly modern. Style and fashion had so completely changed that they created a drastically different backdrop for day-to-day living from what had gone before. Clothing was more streamlined, looser, more comfortable, and more practical. And design unfolded in a similar way.

In the late nineteenth century, American homes were shrouded in uber-traditional darkness. Victorian taste leaned toward the macabre, with gaudy wallpapers, strong and muddy colors, and heavy furniture. In my view, this was one of the least attractive styles in history, and it seems inevitable that both the Art Nouveau and Art Déco movements began as rebellious responses to the fussy Victorian era, the romanticism that preceded them, and

A Karl Springer mirror hangs above a Renaissance-style console with classical detailing.

signaled a commitment to design rooted in craftsmanship and responsive to the innovative ideas that converged from all fields at the turn of the century.

The grand exhibition of 1925, the Exposition Internationale des Arts Décoratifs et Industriels Modernes, was dedicated to living in the modern world. This exhibition generated the term Art Déco to describe design in terms of a broad decoratively modern style, characterized by a streamlined classicism and faceted, crystalline structures, embellished with decorative references to the sleek and the exotic. Designers began using new materials such as rare species of wood, as well as shagreen, alabaster, ivory, and horn. The latter were inserted as trims in desks, tables, and cabinets. Mirrors took on a new look with interesting frames again composed of rare woods and intricate marquetry; lighting was no longer an electrified candlestick or sconce, but a completely new creation often consisting of molded glass or plaster.

Craftsmanship was superb, in keeping with centuries of tradition but viewed as if it had just been discovered. The designs of Emile-Jacques Ruhlmann, for example, were not only beautiful in line and in material, but they exhibited such superb craftsmanship that only the extremely wealthy could afford them. Even today, they command very high prices at auction. Ruhlmann must be considered an artist as well as a genius. His early designs in cabinetry were influenced by the Art Nouveau and Arts and Crafts movements. Through his foray into what would come to be known as Art Déco, largely due to his very designs, Ruhlmann himself created a new look, one that was heavily influenced by neoclassicism. A combination of pure and perfectionist design, rare materials such as onyx and ivory, and master craftsmanship created a new design aesthetic but one that was still in keeping with the tradition of eighteenth-century and earlier cabinetmaking. His clientele was the crème de la crème, and his pavilion at the Exposition was the highlight of the show. Since old-world craftsmanship was the norm for all designers, many specimens of cabinetry of the period have survived

in excellent condition. This movement was long and strong, and it lasted until a new war, a failed economy, the advent of mass production, and the development of new materials such as plastics and Formica brought about its demise.

Designers of the time emerged as rising shining stars, whose ideas may have followed the trends of "modern" living, but whose designs were so revolutionary that one could not help but notice them. These designers may have dropped out of the limelight while the world was focused on wars, international tensions and recovery, but they were only dozing and today they are revered, emulated, and copied.

Who were these champions? Jules Leleu, Jean-Michel Frank, and Jacques Adnet, to name a few in addition to Ruhlmann. Jules Leleu, popular during the Art Déco period, is a name that has come back strong in the new millennium. While less well known today than some of his contemporaries, he was a master craftsman, much along the same lines as Ruhlmann. It was a family business, and in his day Leleu was awarded honors and prizes including one at the Exposition itself. He was a prolific producer of fine furniture of exquisite woods, inlays, and marquetry.

Jean-Michel Frank played a somewhat different role in design. He was the consummate interior designer. Embraced immediately by the haut monde, a phenomenon that only occasionally occurs in design, Frank designed homes, interiors, and showrooms for the Noailles family, Cole Porter, and Elsa Schiaparelli. He was less concerned with cabinetry than with the total décor. But, like his contemporaries, he was excited by interesting and unexpected materials such as vellum, parchment and flat sheets of wood on walls, shagreen and plaster, straw, terracotta, and mica. Frank did not have a long career, but his influence is evident in the work of many designers of the twentieth century.

Today a myriad of books tout these talents and dozens of designers copy them. Why? Because their designs were livable, handsome, of the highest quality, and suited to "modern" life. But if they were so terrific, why didn't they "live on"? Perhaps because the second half of the twentieth century brought many sociological and mechanical changes, and décor changed as a result.

Today, after a rapid succession of design changes in the last thirty years, from traditional to modern and back again, the new generation of homemakers is in search of a clean, calm, soothing atmosphere, modern in philosophy but traditional in value and quality. These days, a contemporary, less cluttered, yet sophisticated environment is what everyone seems to be clamoring for. The contemporary part is evident, but how does one inject the sophisticated part? Designs of the early twentieth century satisfy that agenda perfectly.

The new millennium is not the first time that these designs have made a comeback. In the 1970s, Andrée Putman, Yves Saint Laurent, and Karl Lagerfeld championed all elements of the French Art Déco era. Andrée Putman and Pierre Bergé disagreed as to whether it was she (Putman) or Yves Saint Laurent who brought about this revival, but nowhere was the competition more intense than between Saint Laurent and Karl Lagerfeld—the two competitors who crossed paths in school. And although both giants of fashion came to a similar place from opposite beginnings and with different philosophies, they had at least one thing in common. They were both enamored with Art Déco and they were both acquiring it. Yet, even this similarity was demonstrated in different settings. In the 1970s, Lagerfeld's apartment on the Place Saint Sulpice was decorated in white and black, accented with chrome, satin, and glass, luxury materials all reminiscent of a Jean-Michel Frank interior. Saint Laurent and Bergé also lived in Saint Germain in an apartment that had been designed by Frank for a woman who lived in it for thirty years without touching it. Saint Laurent faithfully restored the apartment as Frank had designed it but introduced elements he loved—the color, the exotic, the outrageous. Marian McEvoy, former editor of *Elle Decor*, pronounced that "the colors were almost edible." Both designers created a great show.

Art Déco flourished commercially at auction and through book sales, and both Lagerfeld and Saint Laurent were at the forefront. But, as often happens in design, this rage was short-lived and by the 1980s, formal French design was back for a long run.

Since today's homeowners have turned away from the fussiness of many French furniture periods, it makes sense to look to a period of design such as Art Déco, a period of the highest craftsmanship, as well as a period of sleek sophistication, angular, and modern in feel. The idea of New French is incorporating classic, clean design into everyday life: A décor and lifestyle that match one another, rather than a fussy stage set, suited to neither young nor mature families.

Creating the New French does not mean using only pieces from the 1930s and 1940s. Designs from the 1960s and 1970s blend well with this new look. Materials such as lucite, goatskin, and chrome, used in designs that were clean and modern for their day, blend very well with furniture from the first part of the century. Designers such as Karl Springer, John Saladino, Baguès, and Jansen worked in materials and shapes that pleased contemporary New York and Paris. These designs are also part of the New French look.

The home is possibly the greatest expression of who we are. While fashions, hairstyles, and youth come and go, our home remains our calling card. While I myself am as happy in jeans as in ball gowns, my home has rarely changed and I am infinitely comfortable there. Whether in New York or elsewhere, my home is the stage I have created for my family to play out the dramas or comedies of their lives, and after many years, I look back and feel I've gotten it right. Someone once said to me, "Your children's rooms look like childhood should feel." I hope my kids agree. Cozy, warm, safe—that's the message I wanted to give to my kids and step-kids.

What I am very attracted to in designing in the New French manner is the idea of taking the best of what's old and what's new and spinning it into an entirely new flavor, just right for the new generation of homemakers. Aside from the basics of furnishings and colors, people's lives are expressed through their hobbies, their books, their collections, their travels and souvenirs, their bibelots and memorabilia. These become the essence of the home. While it can help to have a talented hand to guide, these accoutrements are truly important in defining the home. Often there are small areas in the home that become essential in giving it flair and charm. These may be the least obvious places. A corridor, a niche, a powder room, a kitchen may all be places where the personality of a home is revealed.

ENTRANCES

The entrance gives the first glimpse into the style of a home: is it simple, ornate, casual, or formal? Historically, the entrance has always been a formal space, one that welcomed visitors but also restricted them from the rest of the house. In earlier times, merchants and business associates were received at this point, and the design of the entrance was as opulent as possible. Today, the entrance is not quite so inhibiting. Often one walks right into a space and the home opens up beyond for all to behold. In a multilevel dwelling, the entrance usually incorporates the staircase to the next floor. But, in many homes, the entrance, large or small, is a practical space with seating, some type of cabinet on which to drop the mail, the coat closet, and occasionally the powder room. Although usually tiny in relation to the rest of the rooms, the entrance is surprising complex in terms of the number of elements that go into its design. In addition to the architectural design, flooring, wall treatment, moldings, a mirror, a console, a bench or other seating, lighting, a rug, artwork, and accessories all must be incorporated.

The structural design of the entrance has changed less than that of other rooms in today's home. Its function may have stayed the same, but the interior decorating is different. Since I like the entrance to have a "wow" factor, I often create circular or oval spaces out of uninteresting, generic, square rooms. Walls can be curved, ceilings patterned with moldings, doorways raised or trimmed with large flat casings or even with metal inlays. When this degree of architectural change is not practical, interesting textures, created with paint or fabric or papers, modernize and add architectural elements to the entrance.

Another architectural feature, often overlooked, is the front door. Whenever possible, I create a unique and grand front door. This may be wood, glass, or iron. I draw on all sorts of designs for inspiration. Doors can be enhanced with applied molding, applied metal, or nailheads arranged in a pattern. Occasionally, I upholster the front door. When traditional raised panels are used, the execution can be surprising. Either the placement or proportions are different than expected in traditional design or the molding profiles are new. When using metal, the grill design is crucial and there are many designs from the Art Déco period to draw upon for ideas.

An Art Déco mirror reflects a sinuous Murano chandelier. Walls are finished to resemble stone.

These architectural changes affect the lighting—not only the choice of fixtures but also their placement. A balance must be reached between overhead lighting and wall lighting as usual but their combination may be influenced by other factors such as the wall treatment. This balance can be achieved in a variety of ways, including combining low-voltage lights, LED lights, lamps, sconces, and chandeliers. Midcentury modern mixes very well in rooms where a variety of lighting is needed, as it was common to use sconces with uplights and other "artistic" lighting designs at that time.

The entrance floor is usually distinct from the flooring that runs through the rest of the home or apartment and its treatment can be approached in many ways. Very often this is considered the "special" floor, one that should be marble, stone, or mosaic. Floors may either be a classic French pattern, as marble or stone with corner cabochons, or an entirely new design influenced by the patterns and lines of the 1930s or 1940s. Fresh as that may look today, it is actually a traditional design motif coming out for another airing. The floor can have an updated feeling even if it is laid in wood. Classic wood can be installed in a different pattern, or antique, reclaimed wood can be utilized to create a fantastic old-world look. Wood may be used as the flooring throughout the rest of the home, but the entrance is set off as having a style of its own.

The entrance is an interesting amalgam of the practical and the aesthetic. Important in that it gives its audience the first glimpse of the home, it also houses many functions. The entrance sets the tone for things to come. What gives the entrance the New French style is the combination of traditional elements with motifs taken from the Art Déco period and midcentury design or with contemporary interpretations of classic French designs.

The Art Déco–inspired floor pattern, created from traditional marbles, adds grandeur to this apartment. The brass center medallion, a classic motif, anchors the starburst design.

OPPOSITE

Creating an oval space out of a rectangular entrance adds glamour to this apartment in a modern high-rise building.

ABOVE

Antique, reclaimed wood set in an Art Déco–inspired pattern combines traditional and contemporary in a typically New French design.

RIGHT

Colorful turquoise walls mix with a 1930s mirror, a whimsical chandelier, and a classic directoire center table.

A pair of Lucite columns was used to create a console table in an oval foyer. The glass top was molded to the contour of the room.

OPPOSITE

The painted plaster walls present an unusual wall treatment but are subtle enough to serve as a backdrop for modern art. The sterling silver reveal adds both architectural interest and provides a molding from which to hang pictures.

LEFT

A classic Parisian door inspired this design. The wood is painted and trimmed with nailheads. The knob is centered, a very French detail. Above, the shirred fabric is a gesture to centuries of tented ceilings.

OPPOSITE

The sterling silver reveal brings a touch of brilliance and luxury to this entrance and complements the singular painted walls. The benches are shagreen and the lighting is midcentury.

OPPOSITE

Art Déco–inspired furnishings—chandelier, bench, and table—complement the rectilinear pattern of the paneling in this house in the Hamptons.

RIGHT

Luxurious period Art Déco light fixtures, console, mirror, and benches set the tone in the entrance and the adjacent solarium of another Hamptons house. Antique-style limestone flooring completes the look.

Sometimes the original architecture of a house or apartment presents a panoply of traditional elements. Here the intricate eighteenth-century-style detailing was softened with a floor design that is classical but geometric and a simple but massive chandelier whose shape says it all. Sculpture by Jedd Novatt echoes the iron banister and window grilles in a modern statement.

An entrance can serve multiple purposes. Here the small space serves as a passage into several different areas. In order to avoid a space overburdened with doors, simple, unframed openings give the entrance a modern architectural feel, which contrasts with the traditional parquet floor and molded baseboard. A Chinese console adds to the mix.

Entrance doors can be enhanced with a bit of "cosmetic surgery." In both cases, only one door opens to the public corridor, but on the interior the faux leaf gives the illusion of grand double doors.

This entrance combines traditional late-nineteenth-century sconces and a mahogany center table with modern art, an alabaster disk chandelier, and a timeless zebra rug. The Botero figure comes to life in this setting and seems to be observing the room.

Traditional elements mix with the whimsical and unexpected, such as the *bois doré* fluted pilasters turned into standing lamps. The traditional center table in dark walnut and the painted boiserie chandelier stand out in this rotunda, marked by a modern take on a stone floor and equally modern, streamlined moldings.

A variety of flooring options: marble, tile, and reclaimed wood.

LIVING ROOMS

In France, the living room is called the salon. The names of other rooms reflect their function—the *salle à manger* for the dining room, the *salle de bains* for the bathroom, the *salle de jeu* for the game room, and so on. But the living room is simply the salon. From the beginning of the twentieth century until the late 1950s, artists, writers, and philosophers gathered at the storied Parisian cafés of the time—Flore, Deux Magots, and Lipp. But they also frequented the salons of the trend- and style-setters of the same period, and the word took on a second meaning. The salons of the day were gatherings, often lasting for hours and hours, at the homes of the celebrated *monde* of the time—figures such as Gertrude Stein and Alice B. Toklas, to give just a few examples. Salons were places to gather, be very comfortable, eat and drink, and above all think and talk. Being included was important, but being sought after as host or hostess was even more important. A comfortable décor was paramount in creating a popular salon. The salon was clearly the greatest room of its day.

When designing a living room today, it is very important to consider its use. All too often, living rooms have been seen as a calling card, a place to show off, to be proud of, to be sure, but a "look but don't touch environment" that was rarely used. While it is important to design your home to reflect not only who you are and who you would like to be, it may even be more important to design a room you can use! In the last ten years, people have taken to calling their living room the "great room," an odd choice at best. A living room, by any other name, is still a living room. It can be small and intimate or large and palatial, but it still is the room which was created for people to live in. A home at its most basic is comprised of a living room, dining room, kitchen and one or more bedrooms. In this case, the living room becomes the most important room in the home as its title suggests: the room in which the family really lives.

The living room contributes greatly to the tone and style of the home. However, whatever style influences the décor, the most important consideration is function. How to begin? First prioritize your furnishing needs: Do I want a piano? Do I need a desk? A card table? An entertaining or dining area? Should there be multiple seating areas? Where will we be watching TV? Once these decisions are made, a floor plan can be developed that takes into account both the proposed program and physical elements such as the view, the lo-

OPPOSITE AND OVERLEAF

Although clean and modern architecturally, the overall look of this room is softened with traditional and midcentury accessories.

cation of the fireplace, or any structural restrictions. The plan must then be filled in with sofas, club chairs, banquettes, chaises and other seating, and soft furnishings. In the New French mode, this seating category is filled in with contemporary silhouettes. The fussy, tufted but uncomfortable seating of the early twentieth century gave way to sleek seating trimmed with wood in the 1920s and 1930s—modern but comfortable and opulent. These in turn gave way to hard-edged bare-looking sofas in the middle of the century. But today, a contemporary silhouette marries sleek straight lines with plush cushions and thick, inviting, shaped upholstered pieces, the best of both designs.

Elements such as architectural detail, color palette, wall coverings, floor coverings, both architectural and decorative, are added into the mix. In studying the décor of the early twentieth century, one can see the dramatic change between walls of that period and how they were designed formerly. Paneling, perhaps the most basic traditional element, was suddenly radically different. Wide planks of honey-colored and other light-toned wood, in species never thought of before, adorned salons and living rooms in the cosmo-politan cities of the world. Large pieces of shagreen, stingray skin, or *galuchat* were cut into squares and glued onto walls. Parchment was also used as a sophisticated wall-paper, again cut and applied in squares or other shapes. The total lack of pattern, even color, was a radical shift from what existed before. Period photographs show the mold-ings completely removed from the formerly traditionally adorned homes. Today, attrac-tive wall treatments are an integral part of New French design in that they surround the furnishings with a sort of "canvas" or stage on which the furnishings become the actors.

A parallel design revolution occurred in the arena of case goods, or wooden furniture, such as coffee tables and cabinets. Cabinetmakers such as Ruhlmann and Adnet worked with precious materials that were never considered for such uses before. The combina-tion of straight lines and form that was tied very strictly to function and luxury, created furniture that was to be, in short, simply gorgeous. Since this period was only seventy to eighty years ago, many pieces survive, and today's designer is lucky enough to have a panoply of furniture and accessories available.

Draperies have also evolved. Throughout many periods in history, draperies have gone from over-the-top frills and pomp, replete with cord, fringe, and other intricate passe-menterie, to simple straight panels with nary an *embrasse*, or tie-back, in sight. Although draperies were originally functional, protecting rooms from drafts and light, today they play an important decorative role. Draperies and blinds add texture and even architectural definition to a room and complete its look and style. Heavy silks and satins, brocades, florals, damask, or chintz, have given way to sleeker materials. Taffetas, cottons linens, and duchesse satin, and for the most part solids, stripes, or modern textures have become the fabrics of choice. Trims, such as cords, moss trim, and tapes, finish them off in a tailored way, and metal tie-backs or simple cords, hold them back. In France, both traditional and modern draperies tend to be plain, a design element often misinterpreted in French-style interior design in the States.

Lighting has changed as well, but it is less about placement and more about the fixtures themselves. The New French incorporates lighting from the entire twentieth century, and lighting from the 1950s, 1960s and 1970s mixes very well with the simpler look of today. It has a clean modern look. Even when crystal, they tend to be geometric and angular and avoid the cascading crystal look so often associated with French interiors.

Patterns and textures are the predominant features to be considered when selecting rugs for living rooms. A modern décor looks fantastic on a traditional Aubusson or oriental rug, but there is also a vast selection of new and fresh carpet designs. There are combinations of textures never grouped together before. These are wools mixed with jute, sisals mixed with linens, wools mixed with silk. Patterns vary from busy tone on tones or solids with luxurious solid borders—almost too many from which to choose.

The traditional can still prevail around the fireplace. The beginning of the twentieth century did not do much with fireplace design. With the advent of the Art Déco period, only the very wealthy could remove their century-old mantels and create a modern masterpiece à la Jean-Michel Frank so apartment-dwellers in France usually kept their nineteenth-century mantels. Today, traditional marble mantels still abound in contemporary settings. As with moldings, the traditional French architectural features are strong and numerous; they are simply accepted. When a cleaner, more modern look is desired, the mantel can be replaced with a bolection type of mantel or a new form can be created. Whether the mantel is contemporary or traditional, the accessories have a new look. There are wonderful andirons and fireplace tools all through the twentieth century from the 1930s and 1940s and equally fantastic ones created today by contemporary designers and vendors. Déco-inspired motifs can be found on andirons and fireplace tools and screens by mixing metals, or adding glass and other ornamental trims. The latter part of the century produced andirons with Lucite trim and wild designs, often with matching tools. Fireplace screens lean toward glass or glass trimmed in metal, or just a mesh screen for protection with no ornamentation at all. Today, the aesthetic beauty of the fire itself and the mood it creates is the focus rather than the physical warmth of yesteryear.

There are also the accessories that dress the mantel shelf. Modern art or sleek Déco-inspired mirrors, mirrors from the 1970s or mirrors crafted in Murano add to the contemporized look. While classic French dictates porcelain garnitures or clocks with matching tazzas, today sculptures, frames, bowls, and vases can create a still life on the mantel.

The New French living room cannot escape its traditional roots no matter how modern it might be. Very often, what seems to today's young home dweller to be new and different, is simply a floor plan of the utmost classic design and proportion that has lain dormant through a generation of house design. The sleek walls and moldings, handsome but stark draperies, straight-lined upholstery dotted with lighting, tables, cabinets, and accessories from the 1920s to 1940s combined with those from the 1960s and 1970s create a new recipe for a modern living room.

OPPOSITE AND OVERLEAF
Here is a mélange of old and new. The immediate impression is traditional, but note the Art Déco scones, the clean-lined ottoman with a geometric Greek key design, and the modern nailhead-trimmed club chairs as well as the classic center table designed with striped Déco-inspired marquetry.

The clean lines and translucent glass of these pendant fixtures contrast with the sparkling crystal of traditional chandeliers.

RIGHT, LEFT, AND
OVERLEAF

This room exemplifies the
essential eclecticism of the New
French interior. The walls are
dressed with traditional, but
plain, moldings and painted in
pale grays and white. The sofa
is whimsically colored in
turquoise leopard. The Louis
Vuitton trunk and handsome
Regency-inspired bookcase
add texture, while the Matthew
Pillsbury photograph and the
set of four 1930s French silvered
ceiling lights offer a modern
touch.

The Carrara marble mantel
evokes those found in grand
nineteenth-century Parisian
apartments. It is dressed
with a 1970s glass firescreen,
an Art Déco bronze clock, an
eighteenth-century Murano
mirror, and Italian *bois doré*
scones. The surround is upholstered in white ostrich.

Neutrals float against a background of golden
Venetian plaster. Paint and plaster were mixed,
applied, and buffed numerous times to achieve
a glow. Contemporary upholstery styles mingle
with Art Déco lamps from Carlos de la Puente,
chinoiserie cocktail table, and modern art pieces
such as bronze sculpture table by Jedd Novatt.

Traditional moldings are angular and mix with any style. Here modern accessories punctuate the classic shapes of the sofas, which are covered in stark white cotton duck fabric.

OVERLEAF

This Hamptons living room is clearly inspired by the early 1930s and 1940s in France, but it incorporates a traditional, though streamlined, fireplace, a 1970s coffee table, and Karl Springer mirrors as well as traditional Ralph Lauren club chairs.

These classic limestone mantels are conservatively accessorized with traditional tazzas and an Art Déco–inspired screen (right) and Italian Art Déco vases paired with traditional andirons (left).

While still a very important feature, both in look and comfort, the fireplace is now dressed in a less cluttered, spare way. The andirons are bicolored and modern.

This living room mixes contemporary furnishings with traditional architectural features, such as the coffered ceiling, panel moldings, and herringbone parquet flooring. The space is divided into two distinct living areas—one by the window and the other near the fireplace—by a back-to-back sofa.

The clean lines and richly grained wood of the Biedermeier-inspired desk add to the New French look. Biedermeier, although early nineteenth century, coordinates very well with all modern styles. The collection of boxes, both shagreen and burlwood, contrasts with the group of inkwells and the English brass ring frame.

In this glamorous living room with panoramic views, the goal was a soft, contemporary look. Classic sofas mix with simpler designs while the case furniture includes both Art Déco and Chinese pieces. The ottoman, or pouf, is contemporized with a Greek key design. Dressmaker detailing, seen on the lampshades and the overscaled bullion trim on the slipper chair, adds to the luxurious feeling.

DINING ROOMS

In France the *salle à manger* approaches holiness. All the world is aware of how the French revere food and dining. There can't be anything more traditional than the French relationship to preparing and serving food. Dining, and dining properly, is a national pastime. Not only are long hours dedicated to the process, both the preparation and the enjoyment of, but the concept takes priority over work, television, and Blackberrys. I can't count the scowls I've received for Blackberrying à *table*. Whether in the home or at a restaurant, mealtime is sacred, a time for enjoying life and friends.

It is unusual not to find a dedicated dining room in Parisian apartments, as most were built during eras when traditional morés reigned. It's no wonder that for centuries the French have been world leaders in luxury tableware and cookware. Table top, as we refer to it in the States, is referred to as *les arts de table* and *art de vivre* in France, where it truly is the art of living, or the well-lived life. Centuries of experience and training have rendered the French *femme au foyer*, the consummate hostess. And, much like that genetic flair for tying a scarf, the French find this effortless. There is almost no distinction between a special dinner and "just" dinner. I have time and again watched my French friends serve a meal that has been lovely, entertaining, and delicious in every way, with the utmost nonchalance. Although I think I set a pretty mean table and wow them every time, I cannot say I am nonchalant! There is a gift to being able to devise a perfectly balanced menu that looks great, tastes delicious, and leaves the guests happy. I have always enjoyed entertaining, even in my teens, and my style has certainly evolved over the years. But, while twenty years ago, I produced everything *en croûte*, today I have pared down my cuisine as well as its surroundings. Food certainly goes through trends, and today's food fashions pair well with the New French. The trend is toward "slow food" or Le Fooding. Food is simpler, down to earth, taken from the *terroir*, and the dining room in turn has become simpler as well.

While dining rooms, composed of tables, chairs, and chandeliers, could be considered simple because their function is so well defined, they can still run the gamut of décor in their execution. Replete with crystal chandeliers, gilding, and ornate "Louis everything," a dining room can be overbearing, and often it is. Since modern life calls for fewer formal dinners, and a dedicated dining room is often considered a tremendous luxury, its décor

A pair of glass panels, found in the Marché aux Puces, become a swinging door to this Parisian-inspired dining room.

has sobered up dramatically. The same elements that were used in opulent dining rooms can create a serene oasis, still elegant but more casual.

Some of the loveliest furnishings produced in the 1920s, 1930s, and 1940s are well suited to today's dining room. Sideboards, buffets, lighting, and screens designed and fabricated during that era are abundantly available today. A buffet from this period is not only practical, in that it was designed for "modern living," but so handsome that it serves as a focal point of the room as well. Sideboards in the eighteenth century started as tall cabinets open on the top and closed below known as *buffet à deux corps*, in England as a dresser, in the United States as a hutch. Later this sideboard was reduced to a chest or cabinet of sorts, heavy and closed, and finally to something more delicate and elegant. When the designs of the 1930s became popular once again, sideboards transitioned into practical storage cabinets with a certain heaviness that evoked Déco period pieces crafted from rich and exotic woods, metals, and precious materials. There are many stylish examples of buffets and cabinets, both Art Déco and midcentury, that are suited to today's dining room. Dining tables and large sets of chairs are much more difficult to find. While it is certainly not necessary, or even preferable, to match the dining room case goods to one another, one would strive to find a table and set of chairs that would complement the pieces in the room. It is often necessary to have the dining table custom made, especially if there are special sizes to be accommodated. There are certainly wonderful 1920s and 1930s dining chairs to be found but the sets tend to be quite small, and reproductions are sometimes the answer.

Beautiful dining furniture is the first step, but the surrounds are what really create the mood. People are tired of fussy interiors so walls and windows have become more plain in design, color, and pattern. Texture and materials have become more important in much the same way that new wall coverings, such as skins and fabric, were in the 1920s and 1930s. I find myself drawn to the unusual when developing ideas for walls. I search for unexpected materials in much the same way as my twentieth-century colleagues did. I have covered walls with wood veneers, fabrics cut into squares, and, in fact, all types of papers, fabrics, and materials used in unusual ways. I have used glass, *eglomisé*, and foil squares, shagreen, stenciled, plain, and woven leathers, even newspaper and sheet music to create interesting walls. Of course, I have used woodwork as well—such as Art Déco–inspired applied moldings, wainscoting, and lattice, utilized in some unique way, a way I hope, that has not been thought of previously. I have mixed materials, incorporating slats of wood with stone or tile. Paneling walls and switching the material unexpectedly can create a newness, a freshness. But occasionally, even when I am trying to create a modern look, I leave opulent traditional moldings. In every instance, it's the mix that determines the outcome.

Dining rooms can be tricky when it comes to flooring. A bare floor can sometimes appear too cold, too unwelcoming, but a dining room floor must be practical. I always opt for stone or wood when specifying a dining room floor. I stay away from politically correct, fashionable

While a Parisian *salle à manger* would once have been dressed to "the nines," this table is elegantly set with Royal Copenhagen china and Biot bubble glasses. These are inherently less formal, yet the overall effect is sophisticated and inviting.

floors such as bamboo. Like them, I do, but not for dining room wear. I gravitate toward more practical choices when a floor is heavily used. Rugs can soften and add an entire dimension to the mix, but one must be very careful when it comes to carpeting of any type. The New French look dictates a sober rug, but practicality suggests darker colors or more patterns. One way to achieve this is with texture. As more and more European and Far Eastern suppliers are explored, there are more and more choices available in the market. The incorporation of silks and linen threads mixed with wool create exquisite concoctions that are at once both new and fresh and as traditional as can be. Another way to incorporate pattern is to use a solid field, preferably with a darker center field, with a wide border in a lighter color. The rug looks cool and forward, but the practicality is maintained.

Les arts de table is practically a national pastime in France. Since cuisine is so important in French culture and French daily life, china, crystal, linens, and cutlery are very much in public awareness. Internationally known brands such as Christofle, Puiforcat, Baccarat, Saint Louis, Raynaud, Bernardaud, Ercuis, Val Saint Lambert, Biot (the list goes on and on and on) are everyday names. In France, almost every household has at least one knife from Laguiole, the world-renowned village for cutting-edge cutlery. With sets of dishes being handed down from generation to generation, the French give great thought and much energy into designing table settings. On the one hand, it is a natural talent, but on the other hand, it is approached as a process. Not merely china, crystal, and cutlery, but also candlesticks and candles, nut dishes and accessory dishes, centerpieces, epergnes, garnitures all go into making a beautiful table. The French design their tables not only with the practicalities of the menu in mind, but also with consideration as to how to entertain and create atmosphere for their guests. Since often one or two sets of china may be all the hostess collects, it stands to reason that using them in a new way would be refreshing.

In creating a new look from scratch, it would be easy to choose from a vast array of simply designed china patterns and glassware but a hostess can combine her own more traditional china with simple candlesticks and linens and add streamlined modern or Art Déco serving pieces to create an updated look. Often, just changing the table linens can give a fresh feeling to the design. I am a lover of hard placemats—placemats made from wood displaying some type of design as is prevalent in Europe. Today these placemats are made in every color in a vast variety of textures including faux shagreen, faux ostrich, faux lizard, and so on. An ornate china pattern placed on a plain mat is instantly refreshed. I have never been a fan of tablecloths. For starters, they cover up beautiful tables! I also find them dowdy and difficult to maintain. In general, I use placemats, from the wood-based English-inspired ones to beautiful placemats in every kind of fabric and texture.

A vintage Art Déco chandelier from Paris is the focus of this dining room. Contemporary tableware contrasts with the classic wainscot and cornice in the room.

Table settings today make gestures to everyday living and are whimsically inspired. Here Chinese dishes are juxtaposed with turquoise service plates and Baccarat crystal (right) and Raynaud Limoges dishes with tulips, apples, and tumblers (above).

A monochromatic palette gives the hostess carte blanche with the table settings. In this case, color adds to the overall feeling created by the Chinese dinner-ware and elegant Baccarat crystal. Sophisticated yet extremely cozy, this dining table with its built-in banquette allows the hostess to seat ten and still have the room open to other uses.

The sleek, expanding circular table, with its inlaid parquet, and the crocco-covered tub chairs create an elegant but not overly formal feeling in this dining room. The absence of draperies allows generous views of the terrace and city.

The buffet, one of a pair, is simple and functional and serves as a counterpoint to the Sam Francis painting above it.

Glass-paneled doors provide a view from the corridor into the dining room in this high-rise apartment, where contemporary and traditional elements happily combine. Both these doors and those on the cabinet at the left were created from reclaimed doors of old French cabinets, and the pointed arches evoke the historic Gothic tradition. This simplified form complements the contemporary dining table designed by Nancy Corzine.

This marble-topped buffet is simple and sleek with an Art Déco period tray, classic tazzas, and mirrored sconces that are at once traditional and today. The macassar frame of the drawing adds a dash of exotic wood.

PRECEDING SPREAD,
RIGHT AND LEFT

How to create an elegant, formal but infinitely usable dining room for a young family? Mix handsome Gracie designs painted on silver tea paper with contemporary custom table, vintage midcentury chairs, and Art Déco accessories.

OPPOSITE

White walls always look fresh. Here an eclectic mix of furnishings in a variety of dark finishes is set off by the white walls.

ABOVE

A mix of traditional and contemporary tableware: china from Bernardaud, William Yeoward crystal, and tumblers from Christofle.

Silver in any size, style, and function enhances the New French look.

LIBRARIES

A library is a true luxury. The library may be a room for the family to get together or it may be a formal entertaining area, albeit more relaxed than the living room. The library usually contrasts with the living room in that it is smaller and more intimate. While living rooms are often decorated in light palettes, libraries tend to be darker, replete with wood paneling or dark upholstered walls. The library tends to be an elegant jewel, a place for an intimate drink with friends, reading by the fire, or cocktails before dinner.

Even the word library conjures up something traditional, a sacred place where books were kept and read, a wealthy man's lair. Classic libraries were encased in wooden bookcases, often with carvings and elaborate woodwork. Libraries were often centered around a fireplace and, depending on the size of the room, a library table filled with large books stood proudly in the center. If the library was particularly lofty in height, a ladder or spiral staircase was used to reach the very highest shelf. A library, after all, was a place to access books. Any walls not covered with books or paneling was upholstered with leather or tapestries and the rooms were cluttered and dark.

Today, even a library can take on a newer feeling. The architectural elements and woodwork used in libraries tend to be altogether different. The woodwork leads the design and tends to be more streamlined. The wood selection is often different from the classic mahogany, cherry, and oak of the last thirty years, frequently replaced with exotic woods such as macassar, rift oak, and maple. When an all-paneled library becomes prohibitive, flannel, felt, tapestry, grass cloths, and faux wood papers can be substituted to create the atmosphere that the more costly wood would produce. The ornate moldings used in decades past have been replaced with clean lines that cove crowns produce and tailored geometric friezes. Recessed panels have all but replaced raised panels. Motifs more angular in feel are gestures to, or direct copies of, Art Déco motifs. These have taken the place of the more traditional such as fluted columns or stanchions with classic capitals or Louis XV carving. Neoclassical details also work with clean modern interiors. The finish of the wood has also been updated, getting very shiny or very matte and often with closed pores replacing open ones.

A luxurious touch is to add a line of metal—brass, nickel, or silver—to the recessed panel frame. Hardware for the bookcases, handles and pulls on cabinets, and hinges follow suit, employing more modern buttons, rope, or 1920s and 1930s French motifs. As hardware

Traditional dark polished wood is juxtaposed with a 1920s French iron chandelier and Fortuny silklights to create a sanctuary for enjoying books.

designs become more modern, there is a vast assortment to choose from. Even the classicists like Guerin and Bricard have all the original Art Déco designs in their archives so it is quite simple to reproduce and order period hardware. This actually begs the question as to whether it is old or new design! In France today, there is a huge assortment of new hardware in new mediums such as, for example, blown glass created on the tiny island of Bréhat. One can also find an abundance of vintage hardware at the Marché aux Puces in Saint Ouen, Paris. Vintage hardware adds a bit of that "we've been here forever" look. Finishes can vary in modern design as well. Whether brass (gold) or nickel (silver tone) is the desired finish, a room of period and modern things often has a combination of finishes.

A bar was often found in the library in the 1920s and 1930s. So popular in the 1960s when socializing at home was at its peak, the bar fell out of favor in the 1980s and 1990s. Today, the bar is once again a popular addition. In France, bars from both the nineteenth and twentieth centuries are popular and bountiful. Gorgeous Art Déco examples are on display in the Marché aux Puces, and bar specialists are available to locate the perfect size. Besides being functional, bars are also extremely attractive, often creating a focal point in a room. The accessories one can collect to adorn them are elegant and witty. Some of the most attractive French objects from the 1930s are cocktail shakers, pitchers, decanters, glassware, and trays, all embellishing an attractive bar. Everyone wanted to emulate the Duke and Duchess of Windsor, who were at the helm of fashion, owning and using simply the best and most fashionable objects of the moment. This period was prolific and creative; makers such as René Lalique, Lanel for Christofle, and others were at the peak of their creativity. Today there is a wide array to choose from, both from the movements' leaders in *arts des tables* and the not-so-well-known. Besides the familiar pitchers, decanters, and the like, there are entertaining oddities from this period. Toothpick holders, napkin holders, coasters in matching cases, and ashtrays also add cachet to bars and bar carts. When the room layout does not allow the space for a freestanding bar, a bar cart is an alternative. Bar carts from the 1930s through the early 1950s exist in many materials and fantastic designs and shapes. They can be made of wood, brass, stainless steel, rope, or leather. They can be stationary or on wheels, or be stationary with sections that pivot outward, creating a layered look. Bar carts correctly accessorized stand out as tiny jewels in a room, and this type of display can be created in the smallest space.

What is a library without books? Today libraries tend to include a combination of leather-bound classics and contemporary art books. For Art Déco furnishings à la mode, monographs of their creators are in demand. When a more modern look is desired, the bookshelves can be designed to accept these very tall books. Interspersed in the bookcase may be a collection of simple frames, trimmed in chrome, exotic woods, shagreen, crocodile, or tortoise. Crocodile frames with a tiny bevel in silver and ivory frames are among Parisian collectibles.

The quintessential 1930s French freestanding bar, so suitable to today's entertaining.

This classic game table is embellished with tortoise magnifying glasses, a crocodile box, and an Andy Warhol print.

Once we've shaken our cocktail and poured it into a Déco tumbler, where can we put it? The cocktail table is a creation of the twentieth century. It simply did not exist before. It is easier to find examples from the Art Déco period than from any other period of design in history until the middle of the century. In pure traditional décor, designers had to be creative with trays, trunks, and *surtout de tables*, but the Art Déco period produced a myriad of low tables in wood, glass, marquetry, inlays, vellum, shagreen, leather, and parchment. Again, tables of this period were creative, sleek, simple, but made with impeccable craftsmanship.

Desks are often found in the library. French desks of the 1930s and 1940s can be found in abundance and come in many shapes and sizes. Desks highlighted the creativity of the cabinetmaker or interior designer. Even when a desk was made of a classic wood like mahogany, it was trimmed with an inlay of ivory, brass, or another wood. The exotic woods could be inlaid with lines of rows of pin dots or marquetry designs. These lines can be straight, but the desk itself may be curved. The designs, once modern and outlandish, are collected and exhibited in museums all over the world, and there are still examples of this work in many price levels. There are wonderful examples of these desks at dealers like Maison Gérard and Bernd Goeckler in New York and in the Carré Rive Gauche and Elcabas in Paris, as well as less costly ones in the Marché aux Puces.

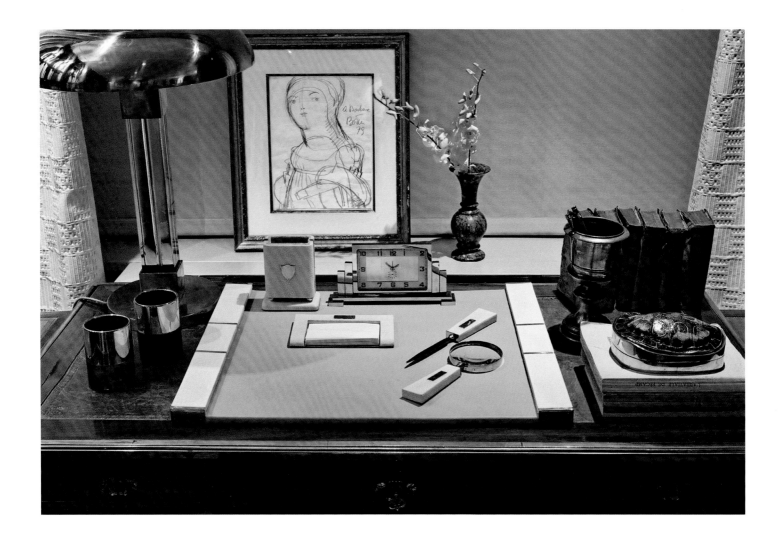

ABOVE

A traditional desk takes on a different look when fitted out with shagreen desk accessories, an Art Déco clock, and a modern drawing.

OVERLEAF

A monochromatic color scheme traverses periods: a classic sofa is paired with contemporary accessories including French linen and leather bookcase lights, a 1920s cocktail table, funky skin chairs, and a painting by Jean Dubuffet.

Among the most charismatic designs of the period are the leather-clad accessories designed by Adnet. His leather-wrapped lamps, standing lamps with small tables attached, magazine racks, and desk accessories are fashionable, practical, and exquisitely designed. Again, Adnet was prolific, and his pieces can be found at auction or from dealers. Often executed in red, green, and black, the leathers are buttery and faded and blend with many color schemes. Leather as a material was innovative and coveted at the time. Jean-Michel Frank created leather club chairs for Hermès with exterior reverse seams, still fashionable today.

In the New French, the library has become clean, sleek, and fresh, but at the same time the room retains its traditional ethos: a cozy, rich, and warm sanctuary.

This library is large and handsome but maintains its coziness. Side tables, upholstered club chairs, and leather club chairs are all vintage Art Déco. The colors are soft and harmonious neutrals and watery blues

This gentleman's library is soothing in cocoa coloring. The standing lamp is an original design by Monique Conil in Paris; the cocktail table was created from a Louis Vuitton trunk.

RIGHT
A Jules Leleu table, shagreen lamp and boxes, a Chinese papier-maché cocktail table, and Holland & Sherry pillows create a modern feeling. The books are covered in vellum calligraphed with the titles.

OVERLEAF
Bars have been in and out of fashion over the last century, but now it seems as though they are here to stay. Beautiful and functional, bars add a focal point to a room and accommodate a vast range of accessories and collectibles.

OPPOSITE

The bar cart is a great alternative to the built-in bar when space is limited. Here a polished mahogany cart holds Baccarat crystal decanters, a 1920s French cocktail shaker, and other useful accessories.

RIGHT

Glassware from Ralph Lauren adds a touch of a British gentleman's club to this 1970s chrome bar cart.

Bar carts add an architectural element to a room. This midcentury chrome bar cart (left) is dressed up with classic accessories from the 1920s and 1930s. This beautiful mahogany table (right) is treated as a bar cart, but could be equally lovely as a serving piece.

The combination of textures and furnishings in this room is unmistakably New French. The walls are covered in woven leather while the upholstery fabrics are soft velvets and crewels. The straight lines of the Chinese-inspired low table and the brass-trimmed end table are modulated by the subtle curve of the arms of the sofa. Color is enhanced by the vivid silkscreen print by Damien Hirst from his Cathedral series.

This bar was created in an ungainly space between
two load-bearing columns. Grain-matched wood
topped with marble now links them with built-in
cabinets behind. Vintage 1930s French barstools
were originally designed for a yacht. Walls are clad
in the woven leather of the main space, but here
are enriched with nailhead trim.

A modern version of a traditional wing chair is covered in blue linen and trim with nailheads. A 1930s-inspired chrome and glass table, Déco-inspired wall treatment, ribbed chenille rug, and burl and ivory box evoke the sumptuous materials of the early twentieth century.

RIGHT

In a room with traditional "bones" the simple window treatment and a Louis Vuitton trunk used as a cocktail table add a modern note.

OVERLEAF

This long, narrow library is divided into two seating groups. Luxurious fabrics include buttery leather, mohair velvet, and duchesse satin, all in deep, tertiary tones for practicality.

However modern the overall look of an apartment, owners want an element of coziness in the library. Here the cabinetwork is clean and bleached gray and the lines of the furniture are straight and structural, but the color palette and personal collections create a warm and inviting atmosphere.

BEDROOMS

Embodying escape from daily work and life, a place to be coddled and to cuddle up, the bedroom has much symbolism. Where recent modern decorating trends had included much in the way of opulent décor, the New French has pared down the pomp of these elements significantly. Until recently, it was not uncommon to swath the bed in fabric, in one way or another. Canopies, either four-poster or draperies swagged against the wall, were created in a variety of ways. Today one sees much less fabric surrounding the bed. Upholstered headboards remain a basic and very practical way to top off the bed, but the preference of styles has changed. These now range from the simplest shape with or without wood framing, to oversized, buttoned, channeled, or sleek, incorporating night stands and sconces or reaching around the bed with integral arms or wings. In this case, the headboard itself becomes functional as well as decorative.

Window treatments have become conservative as well. Draperies have lost a lot of their recent embellishment, and plain, straight panels have become the most sought-after look. It is interesting to know that French homes always used plain tied back draperies as their model. The swags, swirls, and valances used in many "French" interiors were actually a faux-pas. Today trims are subtle, more tailored, and there are fewer of them. The *embrasse* is often metal or an unadorned cord. In certain circumstances, when the architectural design of the window itself is so dynamic that draperies would detract from the look, the draperies are eliminated altogether. But, although the draperies themselves have been simplified, the number of layers is a practical matter and has not changed. A bedroom needs a layer to block light for sleeping and a layer that lets light in for daytime privacy. Typically the result is a drapery, a blackout layer (such as a roman shade), and a sheer layer.

The functionality of the bedroom, like the dining room, dictates the specific pieces of furniture needed. Night tables are typically a necessity, as is some type of seating. Seating and upholstered pieces show off a cleaner line, fewer cushions, and larger and simpler pillows with cords instead of tassel trim. Chaises, although selected with modern lines, are actually a more traditional seating style than club chairs, and they have made a strong comeback. Chaises may be considered traditional conceptually but stylistically can be found to be both sleek and chic. And the idea of an elegant chaise is in keeping with the luxurious sentiments of Paris of the 1920s and 1930s.

In a classic French bedroom, the bed is set in a boiserie surround or draped at the head. Here a gesture to the classic style is executed in a sleek and modern way, with a Picasso linocut, tailored swing scones, and a simple headboard.

During the last twenty years armoires of every possible size, shape, and color were designed to hide the television, but today exposing a flat screen is considered completely acceptable. The irony is that the French have always left their TVs visible. Now the cabinet of choice is something long and low, and the cabinetry of the 1930s and 1940s and even later includes pieces in exactly the right shape and size. Similarly, night tables from these decades have a lot to offer in terms of originality, quality, straight lines, luxury wood veneers, and function.

Carpeting is essential in creating a bedroom that is cozy, soothing, and comforting. The soft luxurious feel of a carpet under bare toes says, "we're in the right place." As in other rooms, in the New French, carpeting is often solid. It may have a texture or weave of different materials, giving some type of pattern in monochrome, or it may be a combination of fabrics like linen or silk. The effect is soft and warm, not an important statement in polychrome, like the patterned carpets so popular in the 1980s and 1990s. The carpet presents a sumptuous background to the rest of the room.

Color, in fact, plays an important role in the overall look of the bedroom. Color and texture, that is. Colors are downplayed; it's extremely common for bedroom walls to be white or very pale. There is a vast array of textured papers in incredible finishes available today; some rival the most intricate and complicated painting techniques. A little sheen goes along way. When color is used, monochromatic color schemes dominate, and pale blues, grays, and greens are among the most popular.

Styles of bedding have evolved as well. People are very tired of making beds. It's preferable to have a duvet rather than a spread, but throws are added at the foot of the bed as a way of dressing it up. Bedding has gotten more tailored as well. Dust skirts, for the most

part, have given way to upholstered box springs. The box springs, in turn, stand on legs, which, in fact, is how the French have always mounted their box springs—once again a traditional touch that appears modern. When a dust skirt is desired, it tends to be box-pleated or flat, with a simple tape along the bottom.

Depending on the size of the bedroom and the amount of closet space, a dresser may be suitable. Once a dirty word in home décor, the dresser now makes a lot of sense as flat-screen TVs need partners and blank wall space is too much of a luxury. Common in the bedrooms of the early twentieth century, they have found their way back in.

In midcentury America, consoles that housed electronic equipment were found in many homes. This shape and style fell completely by the wayside when armoires became the cabinets of choice in bedrooms and hotel rooms. Today, those "out of favor" consoles are exactly the right proportion to complement a flat-screen TV.

Lighting has taken on a new dimension with oversized lamps of Murano glass, lucite, rock crystal, metal, and marble taking center stage. Sleeker shades, often drum shaped or of more angular design, and interesting materials from midcentury have taken over today's lighting look. However, standing and table lamps from Murano have always been incorporated in French décor, even mixed with the most elaborate "Louis" style. Lighting's functionality can be recessed with ever-more modern technical and ecological advances as well as cutting-edge design. While lighting has always been expected on the ceiling, it is now comfortable on the headboard. Hotel-type reading lights may be attached to the bed, a very welcome change for night owls. Sometimes more decorative ones are used, and sometimes the more traditional swing arms, though perhaps sleeker in design, are used, simply showing that there's not just one way to create a new look.

The challenge of incorporating fresh elements of the New French into bedroom design is combining the notion of sleek and simple with the warmth and comfort of home. All too often, the attempt to create a contemporary bedroom yields a room better suited to a design hotel rather than day-to-day life. A careful mix is a must.

OPPOSITE

A peek into this master bedroom from the dressing room reveals a calm oasis from city life. The color scheme is pale and golden. The 1930s French Art Déco dressing table from the Marché aux Puces is paired with a Lucite chair from the 1970s.

OVERLEAF

This room incorporates a traditional coromandel screen with mirrored furniture and Lucite accessories. The classic draperies replete with tie-back *embrasses* and tassel trim contrast with the whimsical ceiling.

This bed is simple and contemporary as are the linens and the bench. The sconces are vintage Baguès. An alabaster dish light complements the circular ceiling molding. The whole vignette, framed by antique wooden doors, was found at the Marché aux Puces.

ABOVE

This ivory lacquer desk holds
a blue Murano glass lamp and a
Chinese box.

OPPOSITE

This mirrored dressing table is
particularly interesting with its
fluted edges and mahogany legs.
Murano perfume bottles add a
bit of femininity.

OPPOSITE

An oasis of luxury and sophistication crowned with an exceptional and unusual Baguès chandelier.

ABOVE

In this his-and-hers bathroom, classic mosaic is combined with modern elements like the molded-glass countertop and midcentury lighting.

The Hamptons life is exemplified by cool, watery colors, mirrored furniture, and comfortable upholstery.

As is typical in French bedroom décor, the bed is fitted into a niche. This sets off the bed and creates the opportunity for extra closets and reduces the need for night tables. The walls are covered in wood-veneer wallpaper with applied moldings, an unusual combination of modern materials employed in a traditional way. The sconces and hanging fixture are finished in nickel, another contemporary element applied to a traditional form.

This bedroom is contemporary but neither dull nor cold. The headboard is channeled leather; orange pillows give an extra "pop."

Solid carpeting, draperies, vintage mirrored commodes, and rock crystal lamps all add to the luxurious feel of this master bedroom. The soft blue and white palette is soothing and inviting.

These two girl's rooms give a nod to "country French" but avoid the over-decorated, frilly interpretation of the past.

Architecture and furnishings
reinterpret the French boudoir:
the woodwork incorporates
geometric motifs; simple tie
backs hold the draperies; the
furnishings are clean and
straight-lined.

RIGHT
The velvet embroidered
headboard was custom made,
influenced by a Déco motif as
are the bed linens. The white
lacquer nightstand is functional
and luxurious.

These two rooms are inspired by French design but executed in a new way. The girl's room has the classic French bed surround with floral upholstery, but the geometric carpeting, tailored bed linens, and color block ceiling bring this look into the twenty-first century. The boy's room creates a daybed effect and shows off a fabulous French Starbay desk and chair.

The classic French bedroom has been reinterpreted for today's living. The lines of the cabinetry are simplified and the ribbon and reed molding slightly overscaled. The headboard is sleek and modern as is the box-pleated dust skirt. An updated Chesterfield sofa completes this timeless room.

KITCHENS AND FAMILY ROOMS

French and American tastes diverge in the kitchen. In France it is very rare to see a kitchen designed with cabinets built in. As a nod to all that has come before, French kitchens are for the most part a mixture of freestanding elements, taken together and adding up to a *cuisine*. The stove, whose craftsmanship is so fine that it could be considered a work of art, stands alone. Dishes, china, and glasses are displayed on open shelves or in glass-fronted cabinets. The refrigerator is rarely hidden or covered by a blind door. Pots and pans may be hung from racks, stacked on shelves, or stashed below the kitchen counter.

The American kitchen has always been defined by built-ins, but little by little we are moving away from that strict formula. More and more, the kitchen flows with the rest of the home. Whether large or small, grand or simple, today, kitchens are beginning to appear more like rooms. Sometimes homeowners make the mistake of designing a kitchen as if it were separate from the rest of the space. If the home is quintessentially traditional, than an ultra-modern kitchen feels jarring. If the home is very modern, a country kitchen feels out of place. Although it is overwhelmingly American, and continues to be so, to have everything built-in and covered, more and more elements are included that make the kitchen more of a room.

Lighting is one such element. We are moving away from recessed lighting in kitchens, with more emphasis placed on chandeliers and a variety of handsome flush mounts or surface-mounted fixtures. Today, a fresher look is achieved with lighting from the twentieth century.

Kitchens can come alive with color. The basic palette of the kitchen should blend with the home, but color can add an accent that may be not be appropriate in a more formal setting such as a living room. Often homeowners are looking for a calming, neutral background color in the kitchen, but want the exciting feeling an accent color can bring. This color can be introduced by paint or tile on the walls, flooring, fabrics on windows and banquettes, and accessories including china and glassware.

The trend is toward the mixture of the old and new. It is not uncommon to use a French *ciment* floor, either reclaimed or new, with ultra-modern cabinetry and accessories. Subway tiles are popular for backsplashes, as are mosaics. Countertops may be marble or stone, glass or slate, lava stone or wood. Is that old or new? Contemporary or traditional? A good

The color palette of pale gray, white, and turquoise is a counterpoint to the outdoor greenery. The floor is a *ciment* tile in a gray, white, and turquoise. The table is turquoise lava stone and the Maison Gatti bistrot chairs are woven resin in gray and white.

Recessed-panel cabinet doors, Chanel-inspired quilted stainless steel, and vintage barstools from the Marché aux Puces set the mood of this kitchen. The floor is reproduction French *ciment* tile.

and practiced eye can create the balance, blending the old with the new. I have combined old menus with modern black cabinets, French *ciment* floors with lacquer, open wine cellars with granite and brick. The overall idea is, besides being practical, to combine old and new elements and stay loyal to the look of the home.

Family Rooms

The family room—also known as the TV room or media room—is primarily a casual space meant for relaxation. Less formal than the library, it is more likely to serve just family members than guests. Family rooms are created first and foremost for comfort, practicality, and entertainment, rather than specifically socializing with others. Sometimes family rooms are combined with other rooms, such as the kitchen or breakfast room; sometimes they are created in the basement or attic. Or there may be just one entertainment room and the concept of library and family room are merged.

Colors in the family room tend to be darker in tone than is typical of the New French. No matter how up-to-date one wants to be, this is still the room for practicality, kids hanging out, and generally making a mess. Textures of fabrics on sofas and chairs and carpeting and rugs must withstand constant use and abuse.

Caution aside, the family room is a spot to be cozy and comfortable and feel at ease. In the New French, that means clean profiles, straight lines, and clear colors. Woodwork can embellish walls, as well as moldings, glass, and other decorative materials that can add style and interest to the surroundings. Textured papers or fabrics with or without modern paneling can create a sensual feeling to the room. Fireplaces and bookcases add an architectural dimension and provide interest. Fireplaces can be sleek and modern or traditional, as can the mixture of furnishings.

In designing a family room, I like to add an element of surprise. This can be achieved by incorporating whimsical items, whether furniture or accessories, or adding architectural details that in turn impact the entire feeling of the room. In either case, the idea is to create something unique, personal, and eclectic. If a space is large, as with a basement, I like to divide the various sections with an architectural feature such as columns and create individual niches for various activities. Nevertheless, in a big space the color should be unified. Although the colors are darker for practical reasons, the color palette, like all in the New French, is largely monochromatic. Individual areas can be identified through ceiling design, with each marked by a different motif. Similarly, changes in floor materials—wood, stone, or area rugs—can define specific spaces.

If the floor is stone, often the case when the family room is adjacent to the outdoors, the floor can be laid in a traditional way or with a traditional stone and then the furnishings can be more modern. On the other hand, if the flooring is laid in a more modern fashion, traditional materials such as terrazzo or mosaic can be used to create something totally "today." Materials of the first part of the twentieth century were so luxurious that today they are often overlooked. In the 1920s it was not uncommon to find floors with fantasy geometric designs made out of exotic woods and sometimes inlaid. I am partial to reclaimed wood and terrazzo, surely new again. A standard wood needs only a clever pattern to look altogether new. A simple, classic pattern surrounded with a border of any type of stone can give the floor a forward look.

Bookcases are practical and house many things needed in the family room. DVDs, games, books, and so forth go in the bookcase, of course, as well as framed photographs and bibelots.

The family room is another room that is likely to hold a bar or bar cart. Bars are one of my favorite twentieth-century rages; they are not only practical, they are also infinitely attractive. Whether bistro-style from an old café or restaurant or a "modern Déco" bar from a boat or home decorated in the 1920s and 1930s, the bars are gorgeous to look at, with superb craftsmanship and flair. Since cocktails were such a prevalent part of socializing midcentury, there are simply dozens of bar carts from that time to choose from. They can be metal, either chrome or brass, or trimmed with leather. Adnet created fabulous designs in leather that are coveted today. The bar cart becomes an attractive, yet practical, vignette.

Televisions, once a decorating no-no, have finally taken their place in the world of interior design. For most, the bigger the better, since the flat screen is the status symbol of the new millennium. Although some are still worried about hiding the TV, others just hang it on the wall and ignore it. As in the bedroom, a long low console, table, dresser, or buffet can be placed below it to house equipment, DVDs, and so on and serve as a surface for serving or for decorative objects.

The cocktail table, or *table basse*, is important to consider in a family room. On the one hand, people want to put their feet up; on the other they need a place for snacks and to serve. Midcentury cocktail tables are commonly made of glass, Plexiglass, and metal, all great materials for retaining their perfection, but often, clients want something a bit cozier. In that case, I often use what my team affectionately calls a "Penny ottoman," something I've used for twenty years. The Penny ottoman is an upholstered ottoman, square or rectangular (or even round) with a center created out of wood, glass, or lava stone. The upholstery can be tufted or smooth, made out of fabric or leather. It can have a drawer below, or a flip-up center for storage. Occasionally, we fit the interior wooden portion for a serving tray that can be lifted out. These have appeared in so many magazines that we've begun seeing copies of them.

This family room has strong Art Déco influences—from the geometric ceiling moldings and handsome club chairs to the period architectural drawings. The abstract chain-link lamps and zinc-topped end tables add to the mix.

Trunks are another popular way of providing a cocktail table. Louis Vuitton and Goyard black-leather studded trunks have always solved the cocktail table problem. Does that make them contemporary or traditional? Their intrinsic practicality—both their imperme-able surface and storage space—make them desirable. Sometimes the perfect trunk will be the wrong height for a cocktail table, but that is easily fixed by adding wooden legs or wheels. Louis Vuitton is so popular that I have covered residential elevator walls and powder room vanities with its toile monogram.

Upholstered furniture may be fabricated with straighter lines, but the family room is the place where comfort reigns. Sofas and club chairs can still be very comfortable even with an angular aesthetic as long as care is taken with the depth of the seats and with the filling and style of cushions. L-shaped sofas, which virtually disappeared in the 1990s, are back, although more for practicality than any other reason. In a space where the number of seats is at a premium, the L-shaped, or sectional sofa with a corner section, makes a lot of sense. Club chairs with partner ottomans and chaises all make appear-ances in the family room. Trim on the upholstery is usually limited to a cord and the skirt

ABOVE AND OVERLEAF
This vast subterranean space was broken down into multiple, smaller areas—bar, billiard room, media room—by varying the ceiling and floor treatments to give each a distinct identity. At the center, load-bearing columns become a handsome colonnade with inviting, casual seating.

has all but disappeared, adding to the tailored look. Very often the fabrics chosen are solid in keeping with the New French look, accented with another solid in a different color.

Family rooms are notable for their relaxed atmosphere. With New French influences, that atmosphere becomes even more so. The feeling is casual, chic, and easy-going which fits with everyday life.

Whatever the room, whatever the location, whether a home or apartment, in the city or the country, East Coast or West or somewhere in between, the goal of successful home decorating is to create an atmosphere that is comfortable, compatible, and coordinated with our lifestyles. A serious look at the type of environment that gives us a sense of well-being and the dedication to surround ourselves with quality that will last will enable us to take on the New French.

The black matte cabinetry puts the modern kitchen in a new light. White glass countertops are chic and practical while the limestone backsplash, Drucker bistrot chairs, and lava stone table are typically French.

LEFT

This breakfast area was created from a hallway in a prewar building. Note the Greek key–inspired motif created from brown grosgrain ribbon on red felt, contrasted with the diagonal bead-board.

OPPOSITE

In the mode of 1920s and 1930s fanciful decoration, a pair of old windows is installed over a scene of the Alps painted by Melanie Lichaa. The client's travels inspired the scene.

In keeping with the overall character of the apartment, modern elements such as recessed paneling, frosted glass, and white glass counter-tops are tempered with more traditional hardware and tile.

This kitchen incorporates modern cabinetry, sustainable flooring, and midcentury lighting and furniture. The banquette is wipeable faux leather.

In the Hamptons, the "country kitchen" look is updated with a neutral palette and stools based on French bistrot chairs.

Powder rooms, like entrances, should be little gems. On the left, the vanity is covered with vintage Louis Vuitton toile and the light fixtures are vintage Murano. On the right, the walls are covered with thick grasscloth, leaving the unusual 1980s Murano mirror and the nickel-plated 1920s French sconces to shine.

Enclosed porches used for entertaining must be designed for practicality as well as comfort and look. The furniture may be edgy but the materials cannot be delicate. Here the ceiling design adds height to the room.

In this family room, whimsical upholstery modulates the straight lines of the sofa. The Penny ottoman is simple and straightforward. A vintage Knoll credenza, stylish early-twentieth-century stools, and shagreen brackets complete the setting for fun and getting together.

SOURCES

Bernd Goeckler Antiques
30 East 10th Street
New York

Carlos de la Puente
209 East 59th Street
New York

Silver Peacock
1110 Park Avenue
New York

Holland + Sherry
979 Third Avenue
New York

John Salibello
229 East 60th Street
New York

Lee Caliccio
306 East 61st Street
New York

John Roselli
306 East 61st Street
New York

Mantiques Modern
146 West 22nd Street
New York

L'Art de Vivre
978 Lexinton Avenue
New York

Sentimento
306 East 61st Street
New York

Frette
799 Madison Avenue
New York

Eric Appel
306 East 61st Street
New York

Center 44
222 East 44th Street
New York

Craig Van den Brulle
192 Elizabeth Street
New York

Argosy Bookstore
116 East 59th Street
New York

Bernardaud
499 Park Avenue
New York

Maison Gerard
53 East 10th Street
New York

Venfield
227 East 60th Street
New York

William Wayne
850 Lexington Avenue
New York

High Style Deco
224 West 18th Street
New York

Casa di Bianco
866 Lexington Avenue
New York

Mecox
257 Country Road 39A
Southampton, New York

English Country Antiques
26 Snake Hollow Road
Bridgehampton, New York

The General Home Store
100 Park Place
East Hampton, New York

Le Douze
12 Rue Jacob
Paris

Espaces 54
54 Rue Mazarine
Paris

Galerie l'Arc en Seine
31 Rue de Seine
Paris

Galerie Jean-Louis Danant
36 Avenue Matignon
Paris

Galerie Makassar – France
19 Avenue Matignon
Paris

Galerie André Hayat
23 Rue de Lille
Paris

Galerie Sylvain Levy-Alban
14 Rue de Beaune
Paris

Hermes
17 Rue de Seine
Paris

Galerie des Lampes
9 Rue de Beaune
Paris

Delisle
4 Rue Parc Royal
Paris

ACKNOWLEDGMENTS

Many thanks:

To my interior design support system: Charles Cohen, Irwin Weiner, David Ruff, Benny Zale, John and Steven Stark, Cary Kravet, Elizabeth Sechrest, Walter Kunzel, Jean-Charles Moriniere, Penelope Rowlands, Wendy Moonan, Agnes Jamora, Shari Stahl, and Maya Foldes.

To my learned and charming editor, Elizabeth White.

To my indefatigable agent, Karen Gantz, whose taste, ingenuity, and talent know no bounds.

To the talented photographers Francis Hammond, Durston Saylor, Marco Ricco, and Matt Wargo.

To friends and family: My husband, Freddy, who loves France as much as I, and our boys Adam, Alex, Benjamin, Philip, Jamie, and Arie, and supportive friends in and out of France: Barbara, Gael, Nina, Emma, Gilda, Vanessa, Deborah, Bonnie, Michelle and Michael, Sima, Alex, Gail, Andrea, Scott and Lizzie, Meera and Marc, Caroline and Guy, Marty and Paula, Nina and Andrew, Carl and Nancy, Keren and Mark, Linda and Peter, Andrea and Ivan, Sylvain, Regis, and Nicolas.

And to everyone at *Architectural Digest*.

PHOTOGRAPHY CREDITS

Francis Hammond: 2, 4–5, 6–7, 10–11, 12, 13 left, 15, 16–17, 18, 19, 25 left, 27, 36, 40–41, 42, 43, 48, 49, 76–77, 78, 79, 96–97, 99, 102, 103, 104–105, 106, 107, 112, 113, 114–15, 119, 124, 125, 136–37, 138, 139, 167, 172–73, 174, 175, 204, 205

Durston Saylor: 13 right, 24, 28, 29, 31, 33, 35 bottom, 37, 44, 46, 51, 52–53, 56, 57, 58–59, 60–61, 69, 80, 83, 98, 101, 108, 118, 120–21, 126–27, 128, 131, 132–33, 140, 145, 146–47, 148, 149, 150, 152, 164–65, 166, 168, 169, 170–71, 176, 178–79, 182–83, 190, 191, 192–93, 194–95, 198

Marco Ricci: 20, 23, 26, 32, 34, 35 top, 67, 70–71, 72, 73, 74–75, 87, 88–89, 90, 91, 92–93, 94, 95, 122, 123, 129, 134–35, 153, 154–55, 156–57, 158, 159, 160–61, 162, 163, 188–89, 202–203

Matt Wargo: 8, 30, 62–63, 64–65, 66, 68, 84, 86, 116, 130, 151, 184, 185, 186–87, 196, 197, 199, 200–201